GETTYSBURG

KIDS WHO DID THE IMPOSSIBLE!

Gregory Christianson

- Contributions by Tom Rutherford and Gerald Christianson
- Watercolors by Tom Rooney • Oil paintings by Dale Gallon

SB

Savas Beatie

California

First edition, first printing

ISBN-13 (paperback): 978-1-61121-399-7
ISBN-13 (ebook): 978-1-61121-400-0

Library of Congress Cataloging-in-Publication Data

Names: Christianson, Gregory, author.
Title: Gettysburg Kids Who Did the Impossible! / by Gregory Christianson.
Description: First edition. | El Dorado Hills, California : Savas Beatie, 2018.
Identifiers: LCCN 2017053024| ISBN 9781611213997 (pbk : alk. paper) | ISBN 9781611214000 (ebk)
Subjects: LCSH: Gettysburg, Battle of, Gettysburg, Pa., 1863--Juvenile literature. | Pennsylvania--History--Civil War, 1861-1865--Juvenile literature. | United States--History--Civil War, 1861-1865--Campaigns--Juvenile literature. | United States--History--Civil War, 1861-1865--Children--Juvenile literature.
Classification: LCC E475.53 .C525 2017 | DDC 973.7/349--dc23
LC record available at https://lccn.loc.gov/2017053024

SB

Savas Beatie LLC
989 Governor Drive, Suite 102
El Dorado Hills, CA 95762
Phone: 916-941-6896
(web) www.savasbeatie.com
(E-mail) sales@savasbeatie.com

Our titles are available at special discounts for bulk purchases. For more details, contact us at sales@savasbeatie.com.

To Liam, Jaden, and Jesse—my three extraordinary blessings.
Love, eternally and unconditionally.

And in Loving Memory of Margie Keyser.

TABLE OF CONTENTS

INTRODUCTION

CHAPTER 1

ONE DAY LIAM AND HIS SISTER JADEN

are amazed to learn that their grandfather, Gerald (left), met Albert Woolson (below), the oldest surviving Civil War soldier, whose statue now stands on the Gettysburg battlefield.

Surprised that they can touch the Civil War in only three generations, the two youngsters set out with their photographer-dad to explore the battle and share stories of **GETTYSBURG KIDS WHO DID THE IMPOSSIBLE!**

*(L-R): **Gerald** ("Grandpa"), **Liam** ("Son"), and **Gregory Christianson** ("Pops") with the **Albert Woolson monument** on Hancock Avenue.*

Albert Henry Woolson *(1847? - 1956) shows his granddaughter, three-year-old Frances Anne Kobus, how he played a drum during the Civil War in this photo from 1953.*

From **GRANDPA** to **POPS** to my brother, **LIAM**—
that's only **THREE GENERATIONS**
to touch the **CIVIL WAR!**

GETTYSBURG KIDS WHO DID THE IMPOSSIBLE! tells the exciting stories of ordinary kids caught in an extraordinary situation—the Battle of Gettysburg, 1863. But they are up to the challenge and perform heroically.

Our young guides, LIAM and JADEN, invite you along on these adventures. Together with witty but sympathetic commentary, they convey a sense of NOW that can help us serve one another as we strive to form a more perfect Union.

So Kids, Teens, Parents, and Grandparents, come along! This book has something for everyone: single-page introductions for each day of the battle and lots of got-to-know facts, all wrapped in a photographic essay of Gettysburg's National Military Park as never seen before. Reflect, honor, learn, and have fun!

INTRODUCTION THE ROAD TO GETTYSBURG

MAY-JULY 1863

GENERAL ROBERT E. LEE AND THE CONFEDERATE ARMY

have routed the Union forces at Chancellorsville, Virginia. They are ready to invade the North for a second time. In June, 1863, they cross into Maryland and Pennsylvania.

Suddenly, sleepy little towns like Gettysburg and Fairfield are filled with Southern soldiers. General Jubal Early passes through Gettysburg on his way to the Susquehanna River, but Union militia burn the bridge.

The new Union commander, George Meade, isn't sure where Lee is. He sends General John Buford and his cavalry to find out. On the morning of June 30 they begin arriving in Gettysburg. They will soon meet Confederate infantry and a furious battle will begin.

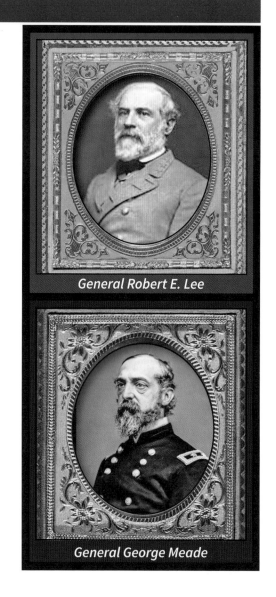

General Robert E. Lee

General George Meade

"Buford's Boys"

Painting by Dale Gallon

JADEN, *something's brewing over there by the* **COURTHOUSE**, *and the battle hasn't even started yet.*

► **UNION SOLDIERS** fought for the **ARMY OF THE POTOMAC** and the **NORTH.** They wore **BLUE UNIFORMS** and were also known as **YANKEES** or **FEDERALS.**

► **CONFEDERATE SOLDIERS** fought for the **ARMY OF NORTHERN VIRGINIA** and the **SOUTH.** They mostly wore **GRAY UNIFORMS** and were also known as **REBELS** or **REBS.**

KIDS

WHO DID THE IMPOSSIBLE!

JUMPIN' JUBAL! GET ON HOME NOW, YA HEAR?!

As **Lee prepares to invade Pennsylvania,** he orders General Jubal Early to advance on York and the bridge over the Susquehanna River. As Early's troops approach Gettysburg on June 26, 1863, they run into the 26th Pennsylvania Militia. This is an emergency militia, a hastily-assembled group of inexperienced citizens, including 56 students from Pennsylvania (now Gettysburg) College.

Early's troops quickly scatter the militia and round up 175 prisoners. They are marched into town and made to stand in front of the courthouse. Toward evening, Early rides up and offers some stern advice. "You boys ought to be home with your mothers and not out in the fields where it is dangerous!"

Early then gives his demands to Mayor David Kendlehart: flour, bacon, shoes, and hats. But the town has little to offer. Next day, the general gathers his troops and departs along the road to York. They'll soon come back!

CSA

GENERAL JUBAL EARLY

What's all the hub-bub about?! I was just getting ready to sleep through **CULLER'S** sermon!

THE LORD BE WITH YOU, BUT TALK FAST!

"**L**et's step it up,"Martin declares, as he urges his horse into a trot. "We don't want to be late for the service."

It is Sunday, June 28. Martin Luther Culler and his friend, Washington Gotwald, are on their way to the village of Fairfield where Culler is to preach. The two young men are students at the seminary in Gettysburg.

"The service is going rather well," Martin thinks to himself as worship moves along. Suddenly he loses everyone's attention. The sounds of tumult are all around the church.

Martin Luther Culler

Horses and shouting! People stand and look out. "Rebel cavalry!" someone declares.

Watercolor by Gettysburg artist Tom Rooney

Abruptly the service ends. Adults rush to the windows. Fearful faces of children press against the glass. Martin, however, can't resist going out in search of adventure. Though still a student, he is encouraged by his sense of importance as a minister-for-a-day.

"Do you think we should be doing this?" his reluctant friend asks as they approach the Southerners who are beginning to set up camp.

Before Martin can answer, shots ring out! From somewhere in the near distance, Union scouts spot the Confederates, fire a volley, and disappear.

"We should have gone back to Gettysburg instead of getting involved," Washington says, as the young men turn on their heels and beat a hasty retreat.

They seek refuge in a friendly home, but angry troopers force themselves in and take the young men out. They're brought before a captain as suspected spies. A terrified Washington is speechless, but not Martin.

"Are you in the habit of arresting men of the cloth?" he brazenly asks.

The surprised officer inquires, "You two boys are ministers?" Not wishing to tell a lie, Martin avoids a direct answer, but refuses to back down.

"Your occupation of the town prevents me from giving the splendid sermon which I intended to preach this evening."

"I've got more important business than to talk all day," the captain thinks to himself. He has other things on his mind, like horses.

"Speak for yourself, *CULLER.*"

"What kind of steeds did you boys ride into town on?" he asks, thinking that he might take them for the Confederate cavalry.

"Our horses, sir?" Culler replies. "We are but poor servants of the gospel, and they are old, blind, and poor in flesh."

The officer laughs out loud. He's heard enough and lets the boys go.

As they mount up and gallop away, Washington shouts, "I've never been so scared in my life! We could have become prisoners or worse." But his words die away in the sound of hoofbeats and rushing wind.

JADEN, *keep your* **CANDY-SNATCHING HANDS** *up where I can see them!*

OH, BROTHER.

Like everyone else, ten-year-old **Charlie McCurdy** has no idea what might happen if the Confederates come to town. The Rebels were surely expected. Charlie's father, president of the Gettysburg Railroad, talks frequently at supper about owners shipping their valuables out of town to avoid the invasion.

Forbidden to leave the house, Charlie itches to go outside as more and more Rebel infantry march into town. When his parents see townspeople leaving their shops and homes and talking to Rebel soldiers, Charlie is allowed to step out the front door, finally!

Surrounded by a sea of gray uniforms, Charlie is swept toward the Town Square. Wherever he looks, townspeople and soldiers are conversing. "Perhaps this Rebel army isn't as fearsome as I thought." Mayor Kendlehart is speaking to a number of mounted Confederate officers. "Nothing interesting here, that's for sure," Charlie thinks.

Heading back towards Chambersburg Street, Charlie spies a large group of Rebel soldiers in front of his favorite store, Petey Winters' Candy Shop.

But Charlie can only look through the window as Mr.Winters quickly sells all his cakes and candies to boisterous soldiers.

Surprised by a tap on his shoulder, Charlie turns to find a young Confederate, his hat full of candy. "Have some?" he asks.

"This invasion is surely not what I expected," Charlie thinks and takes a handful!

▲ *Charlie McCurdy (reenactor)*

◄ *Mayor Kendlehart (reenactor)*

TILLIE SERENADES THE UNION CAVALRY

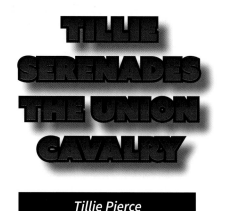

Tillie Pierce

Trying to focus on her reading assignment inside the Young Ladies Seminary, 15-year-old Tillie Pierce is interrupted by a steady CLOP, CLOP of horses too loud to ignore. The sound brings Tillie and her classmates from behind their desks to the windows.

"Here comes the cavalry!" shouts Tillie, "They've finally come to Gettysburg!"

Dusty, saddle-weary troopers on sweaty, snorting mounts appear four abreast along Washington Street as far south as Tillie can see.

Excitement carries Tillie and her friends outside to the corner of High Street and Washington. Crowds of people are lining the street, handing ladles of water, slices of cake, and slabs of buttered bread to troopers pleased by this warm welcome.

Someone near Tillie begins to sing "Our Union Forever," and soon more than a dozen young ladies join the chorus, drawing smiles and salutes from passing cavalrymen.

"Perhaps, just perhaps, the Rebels will learn of our splendid cavalry and bypass Gettysburg," thinks Tillie, as the singing and shouting drown out the fears she holds inside.

OUR UNION FOREVER

WELCOME CAVALRY

OPEN MIC CONCERT ON OUR STAGE THIS AFTERNOON

NOW SERVING!

SONGS · ANTHEMS

Eyster's Young Ladies Seminary

27

CLIMBING THE CUPOLA

TILLIE hopes the Rebs will bypass Gettysburg, but **LYDIA ZIEGLER** sees that they're not!

She would know, **JADEN**. She's got the best view in town!

The arrival of Buford's **Federal cavalry** interrupts everyone's routine. Lydia Ziegler and the whole Ziegler family, five children and two parents, live on the first floor of Old Dorm on Seminary Ridge. Lydia's parents, Mary and Emmanuel Ziegler, take care of the students and the building.

Troopers and horses are everywhere. Officers scurry up and down the stairs of the towering cupola above Old Dorm. No place for a civilian! But Lydia can't resist. As the evening of June 30 comes on, she quietly ascends the cupola. There she beholds a breathtaking view: Union campfires, prayer circles, men singing patriotic songs or writing letters, perhaps their last. And not far off to the west appear thousands of Confederate campfires. Suddenly, Lydia becomes worried.

"I fear what tomorrow will bring," she says to herself.

Lydia Ziegler

As a young Quaker farmer in York Springs, Pennsylvania, Charles Griest is active in helping slaves gain freedom on the Underground Railroad. When the war begins, he must stay at home to care for his mother.

Today, it's June 30, and an urgent message from Pennsylvania Governor Andrew Curtain to Union General John Buford is on its way from Harrisburg to Gettysburg. The governor desperately wants to inform Buford that Confederates are invading Pennsylvania and heading for the state capital.

Hearing shots outside of York Springs, Curtain's messenger refuses to go any further, and accepts Charles's offer to carry the note to its final destination. Even though he could be shot as a civilian spy, he mounts his horse, Lew, and they bolt away.

Arriving near the college in Gettysburg, Charles waves down a Union cavalry officer who immediately sends him to Buford. Impressed by Charles's courage and knowledge of the territory, the general asks him to stay and deliver messages to the troops on Seminary Ridge, Oak Hill, Cemetery Hill, and Culp's Hill. Unfortunately, on July 1, while galloping toward the Union line of battle at what would soon be called Barlow's Knoll, Lew is hit and falls on top of Charles, injuring both.

Amazingly, despite their poor condition and numerous Rebel troops in the area, Charles and Lew survive and make their way back to York Springs. Some years later, Colonel John McClellan, a good friend who arranged for Lincoln's horse when the president came to Gettysburg, presents Charles and Lew with a precious gift for their bravery. "I'm going to give you the cover that I put on the saddle for President Lincoln's horse."

GREAT GALLOPING GRIEST!

Watercolor by Gettysburg artist Tom Rooney

∾ CHAPTER 1 THE DEVIL TO PAY

Dawn—July 1, 1863, 7:30 a.m.

About two miles west of Gettysburg, Lieutenant Marcellus Jones picks up a rifle and fires at Confederate troops. It is the opening shot of the Battle of Gettysburg.

General Buford and his troopers can only slow the Rebel advance. They fall back to McPherson Ridge and the seminary. Infantry under General John Reynolds arrive, but Reynolds is soon killed.

General Oliver O. Howard sees the retreat as he marches into town, and takes up a position just beyond the college. He, too, is overwhelmed. A last stand at the seminary provides time for the remaining Union troops to escape to Cemetery Ridge, south of town. Here they take up a strong defensive position and wait.

The Confederates are victorious. They occupy the college, the seminary, the town, and much of the surrounding countryside. Anxious civilians must flee or spend the night in their basements.

General Buford

General Reynolds

REYNOLDS (standing with horse) arrives at the seminary at 10:00 a.m., quickly locates BUFORD and asks, "What's the matter, John?"

With his cavalry nearly surrounded, BUFORD (hand raised) responds, "There's the devil to pay!"

"Buford and Reynolds"

Painting by Dale Gallon

▶ Few people know that **JOHN REYNOLDS** is offered command of the entire **ARMY OF THE POTOMAC** before Gettysburg. But instead of accepting, this exceptional general persuades **LINCOLN** to allow him to continue alongside his men as a fighting field officer. True to form, Reynolds takes to the field by mid-morning. Thirty minutes later, the Union Army is without its best general.

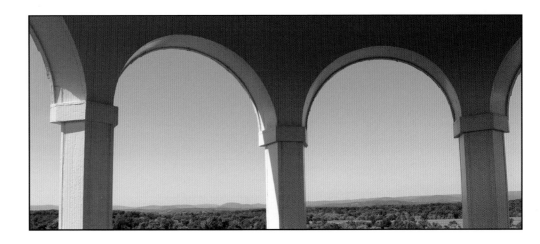

*Views from inside (above) and outside (below) the **CUPOLA** atop **OLD DORM** at the **LUTHERAN SEMINARY***

Desperate defenders form a last stand behind felled trees and fence rails in front of the seminary, providing time for the remaining UNION troops to escape to Cemetery Ridge, south of town.

"Withdrawal of the 151st PA"

Painting by Dale Gallon

▶ **"CAN I FIGHT IN YOUR REGIMENT?"** asks 69-year-old Gettysburg native, **JOHN BURNS.** *"Old man, you better go to the rear or you may get hurt,"* replies the regimental commander. **"HURT, TUT, TUT,"** *Burns responds. Given a rifle captured from Archer's Brigade, Burns fights valiantly on McPherson Ridge, but is hit by* **THREE BULLETS.** *Fortunately, a group of friends find him during the night and carry him home. Burns lives—and because of his bravery walks alongside* **PRESIDENT LINCOLN** *on the way to the Presbyterian Church on* **NOVEMBER 19, 1863!**

John Burns statue

KIDS WHO DID THE IMPOSSIBLE!

To ten-year-old Hugh Ziegler

the arrival of Buford's cavalry is a cause for excitement. Many of the troopers encamp right around his home! Cavalrymen ask boys like Hugh to water their horses in town, or buy knickknacks or something to eat.

On the morning of July 1, a trooper gives Hugh his horse and some money to buy a loaf of bread. Hugh is in his glory! "I feel like a general," he says to himself as he rides slowly and deliberately through town.

On the way back to Old Dorm, everything is changed. Riders fly by in all directions! Suddenly, an officer whacks Hugh's horse on the butt with his saber and shouts, "Hurry up with that horse!"

Hugh, hanging on for dear life, clutches the horse's neck as it gallops back to the seminary.

The trooper is waiting for him. "Get off quick," he commands and lifts the boy to the ground. "Thanks for the bread," he shouts and dashes off to the front.

"What's happening?" Hugh asks himself. To get a better look, he tramps toward an artillery battery on McPherson Ridge. Cannons recoil with smoke and fire! Running back to the seminary as fast he can, the frightened youngster has just witnessed the first cannon shots of the battle.

HANG ON, HUGH!

Watercolor by Gettysburg artist Tom Rooney

The first rifle shots at daybreak sound like firecrackers.

The noise increases with each passing minute. Union infantry arrive, heading for McPherson's Woods.

For Lydia, curiosity overcomes caution again. Slipping from the safety of Old Dorm, she steps carefully through an orchard, just west of the seminary. A barrage of firing stops her in her tracks.

This time the noise is very different. First a buzzing sound, then a *zing! zing!* as real bullets fly by. The Confederates are in the woods!

Turning and running toward home faster than she thought possible, she bursts through the door just as Father shouts, "Everyone, into the cellar, *now!* When Mother and I gather food and belongings, we're getting out of here!" Wounded soldiers stream into the building. Frantic students rush to leave as the seminary quickly becomes a hospital.

Wow! **HUGH'S** hightailing it home and his older sister, **LYDIA**, isn't far behind!

She just might be running faster than her brother!

GO, LYDIA, GO!

"Fighting at the Fringes"

Painting by Dale Gallon

Dan Skelly (reenactor)

Hearing rifle fire since early morning makes 18-year-old Dan Skelly wonder, especially now as the sounds intensify. He leaves the safety of his house for a closer look, and heads across the college grounds toward the Mummasburg Pike.

Clearing the ridge not far from the old Railroad Cut, he is surprised to see lines of gray forming on both sides of the Chambersburg Pike. Some are attacking dismounted

*If **LYDIA** sees the fighting, **JADEN,** the kids in town can certainly hear it.*

Union cavalry, near Herr Tavern. Although firing rapidly, the troopers steadily give ground toward McPherson Ridge. They are even falling back to Oak Ridge where Dan joins a large number of curious Gettysburg civilians.

He climbs a tree and calls down to those on the ground, "I see Union troops coming up from beyond the seminary!" A cloud of smoke passes between Dan and the crowd below. "They're being ordered into the lines near McPherson's Woods," he shouts, "and firing at the advancing Confederates."

Responding to the Union guns, Confederate artillery is louder than anything Dan has ever heard, and causes thick smoke to blanket parts of the field.

The fighting is about to engulf him! Bullets whiz by. Quickly sliding from his perch, he runs down the ridge and away from the noise and smoke.

As Dan cuts through the Sheads property, a Rebel cannonball plows the ground nearby, scattering dirt all over him. Curiosity gives way to fear, and home is where he quickly heads!

UP HERE, GENERAL!

Despite his encounter with an exploding shell

earlier this morning, Dan Skelly goes back to work. He is a clerk at Fahnestock Brothers Dry Goods Store on West Middle Street, just across from the Adams County Courthouse.

As noon approaches, the noise of battle on Seminary Ridge grows increasingly louder. Dan decides to head for the roof above the third floor. He runs up the stairs and climbs through a large trapdoor. From here, he finds that he can't see all of Seminary Ridge, but he can take in the college and the fields to the north.

Suddenly, Dan hears the clatter of hoofs. It's General Howard and his staff, making their way up Baltimore Street and heading directly toward the courthouse. Dan quickly understands that the general wants a view of the battlefield from any high point in town.

Clambering down the stairs as fast as he can, Dan enters the street and invites the general to join him on the roof. Howard accepts, and Dan shows him the way. The general looks over the battlefield with a field glass. Buford's cavalry and James Wadsworth's infantry are heavily engaged with the Confederates.

Just then, a Union officer rides up and addresses Howard. "Sir, I must inform you that General Reynolds is dead. You are now the senior officer on the field."

Even young Dan Skelly realizes the importance of this report. Howard commands all Union forces on the battlefield until other orders arrive.

Dan will never forget how the general keeps his cool. He orders that bands be placed at the head of the XI Corps, and play lively tunes as they march into Gettysburg. Some of the corps will occupy Cemetery Hill as a back-up, while the remainder move north of Gettysburg, just beyond the college.

Unfortunately, this position offers little protection when Confederate General Robert Rodes sweeps in with devastating effect. Despite the outcome, Howard never forgets Dan's quick thinking. In the years after the war, the general frequently visits "Mr. D.A. Skelly," and the two remain close friends.

GENERAL HOWARD loses an arm earlier in the war, and GENERAL PHILIP KEARNEY, who loses one, too, jokes that they can shop together for a pair of gloves! Speaking of arms, I must say that I'm particularly attached to mine!

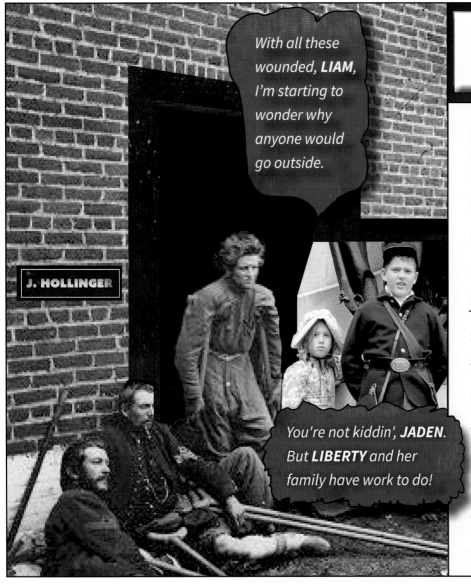

With all these wounded, **LIAM**, I'm starting to wonder why anyone would go outside.

J. HOLLINGER

You're not kiddin', **JADEN**. But **LIBERTY** and her family have work to do!

DESPERATE MEASURES

Ever since they awoke, Liberty Hollinger and her sister Julia listened to the sounds of battle west of Gettysburg. From the porch of their parents' home at the juncture of York and Hanover Pikes, they could not see the flow of Union wounded into Gettysburg that morning. Now they are aware of the steadily increasing noise and troop movements around the college.

"I wonder when Father will return," Julia asks Lydia with worry in her voice. "He left so suddenly after breakfast."

Jacob Hollinger is heading quickly into town. He is going straight to the family's warehouse across from the railroad depot. Even though it was empty of freight, he needed an excuse to get nearer to the activity around the Square.

Turning onto Stratton Street, Jacob is surprised by the Union soldiers at the entrance to his warehouse. Down the tracks to his left, he can see wounded soldiers at the depot and others being helped toward the warehouse. Without a word, Jacob unlocks the building and the wounded begin pouring in. Turning to a medical officer, he promises to return with water and supplies.

Liberty knows from her father's expression that there is serious business ahead. "Father, what is happening?" she asks. His quick explanation is enough.

Liberty Hollinger (reenactor)

"Julia, go get Mother's extra sheets, while I pack a basket of bread, biscuits, and butter. Then we're heading to the warehouse to help."

Returning from the warehouse with her father, Liberty grows increasingly alarmed for their safety as the tumult around the college grows more intense. During the quick walk back, they witness a stream of townspeople leaving Gettysburg along the Hanover and York Pikes. "Should we not do the same?" Liberty wonders, as mounted troopers gallop back and forth across York Street. She knows her father has the same thought, but moving her invalid mother will make travel difficult, if not impossible.

Two Union lieutenants ride up on their way to the high ground on Cemetery Hill. Both officers advise the family to move into the cellar. Gettysburg will soon be overrun by Confederates.

Gettysburg Train Station

Watercolor by Gettysburg artist Tom Rooney

"Can you help us?" Liberty blurts out. Although at risk of being captured, the officers do what Liberty requests. "Mother," she says as they carry her into the cellar, "we'll all be here with you until it is safe to return upstairs."

Coming down the stairs, Liberty steps to the closest cellar window. "Our boys are retreating," she shouts as waves of soldiers run past.

Almost immediately a Rebel flag catches her attention. "The Confederates are here!"

Streams of butternut- and gray-clad soldiers, many stopping to fire, swarm over the Hollinger property. "Now what?!" Liberty asks herself, and quickly backs away from the window.

Little of interest happens in **Gettysburg** that isn't quickly known to 14-year-old Albertus McCreary. Yet the noises he hears throughout this July 1 morning cause him to wonder what he is missing.

Growing sounds of gunfire drift down High Street toward his home. Albertus's natural curiosity gets the better of him. He spots several older friends and their fathers hastening westward to the seminary for a closer look. "Father," he pleads, "please let me go and see what's happening."

David McCreary finally agrees. "You can walk down to the Washington Street corner, but not beyond."

Just one block from his home, Albertus stops at the fence along the Washington Street side of Eyster's Young Ladies Seminary. He is just in time to see thousands of Union troops moving north through town toward the college.

LIAM, can you imagine all those troops marching through town?

Nothing can keep ALBERTUS McCREARY from taking it all in.

ALBERTUS CATCHES THE WAVE

"Those are Howard's men," he hears someone say. Flowing like a sea of blue past Albertus and other cheering onlookers, wave after wave of soldiers move rifles at "right shoulder shift" to ease their quick-march pace.

"Coming to Gettysburg's rescue!" he says to himself, and wonders, "Could any force in the world overcome these magnificent Union infantrymen?" Soon, Albertus will get an unwelcome answer.

"We Have Come to Stay"

Painting by Dale Gallon

SURROUNDED!

Walking home after watching Union troops enter town, Albertus senses that the fighting to the west, beyond the seminary, has decreased. To the north around the college, however, sounds of battle are growing louder and louder. Begrimed Union officers on sweaty horses seem to be riding in every direction—carrying orders, Albertus supposes.

There's also a large number of Union wounded, some walking and others being carried back into town. Albertus overhears conversations about how Christ Lutheran Church and all the warehouses around the railroad depot are filling up with casualties.

Watching from the side porch of his High Street home, he observes a steady stream of wounded flowing toward the First Presbyterian, German Reformed, and Catholic Churches. All fly red flags to show that they have become hospitals. By late afternoon, the sounds of fighting seem much closer. Albertus notices his father's increasing nervousness.

The McCreary family starts an early supper, but it is interrupted when sounds of combat are only blocks away. Following his father from the dinner table to the side porch, Albertus hears a mounted Union officer shout, "Get your family into the cellar. The Rebs are taking the town!"

Albertus notices that the orderly movement of blue-clad troops southward on Baltimore Street is turning into a panic. The Union army is in full retreat, right past his home and right out of Gettysburg!

Everyone dashes toward the cellar. Albertus steps from the porch and throws open the door leading downward. Clearing the last step into the dim, cool cellar, he rushes to a small window and declares, "Here come the Rebels!" Union soldiers are running in front of them. Some stop to fire, some drop to the street, but most are just running.

"Come look, Father," Albertus shouts, "there's a cannon in our street!"

Together they watch it fire, and then disappear from sight down Baltimore Street. For a moment amazement overcomes fear. Albertus has witnessed a scene he could never have imagined.

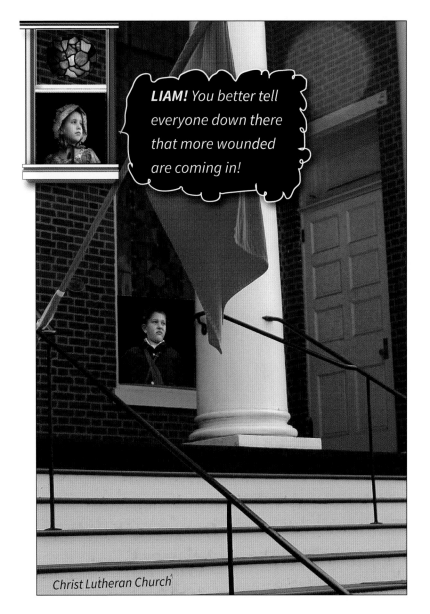

LIAM! You better tell everyone down there that more wounded are coming in!

Christ Lutheran Church

GUESS WHO'S COMING TO DINNER?!

ALBERTUS is having one heck of a day. And it's not over yet!

The fighting has finally passed and sunset nears. Albertus can see Rebel soldiers from his cellar window. Cooking fires are started, and dirty, weary men fall out to rest. But not all.

The loud knock of a rifle butt on the cellar door startles everyone! Albertus watches with fear as Father slowly opens the door to three Confederate soldiers. "Are you hiding any Yankees down there?" he demands, his rifle pointing into the cellar.

"None," replies Father, "just my boys and the housekeeper."

"What about upstairs?" the soldier barks.

"I have no idea," says Father, "but you are free to look about."

The invitation is quickly taken. Albertus hears heavy boots on the floor above. Long minutes pass. Guarding the huddled family, a Rebel sergeant stands nearby.

A dozen Yankees are found. "Who else might you be hiding?" the sergeant snaps. The uneasy silence is broken by the voice of the housekeeper.

"Let's just stop right there! You boys look exhausted and hungry. Let me pass and I'll get us some dinner."

Without seeking permission, she brushes past the sergeant and heads toward the kitchen. Albertus, his family, and a mix of Rebels and captured Yankees settle into whatever seats they can find. Soon, plates of boiled green beans from the McCreary garden appear. They are eaten as fast as they are passed among the men, Reb and Yank alike. Nodding toward the soldiers, Albertus says,

"I'll never forget this Father, the night the Union and Confederate armies joined us for dinner!

Watercolor by Gettysburg artist Tom Rooney

There goes that student preacher, **MARTIN LUTHER CULLER**, racing from the **SEMINARY** again. Like **ALBERTUS**, he has some unexpected dinner plans!

FROM THE FRYING PAN INTO THE FIRE

"**I** thought I'd had enough adventure for one war," Martin Luther Culler declares with concern in his voice. The sounds of battle are coming dangerously close to the seminary where he is a student. "I learned my lesson when I got captured in Fairfield. It's time to leave! I know a family who will take us in."

Martin and a friend make their way from Seminary Ridge into town where they seek out John Winebrenner's home on Baltimore Street. "This will do just fine," Martin says as they approach the door, and are greeted by the family. "We'll be safe here."

But they are hardly settled when the Confederates charge into town. As the Federals retreat down Baltimore Street, the two students join the family in their own retreat to the cellar! "We didn't go far enough away from the seminary," Martin shouts to his friend as they descend.

"Keep it to a whisper," someone from the family instructs. "I can hear Rebels entering the house and going up to the attic. They're probably snipers."

Sleep is difficult as night comes on. The basement is dark and damp, and sharpshooters spend the entire night taking shots at Union forces on Cemetery Hill.

The little band huddles together as the hours pass. Suddenly, there's a loud bang on the cellar door. "We're done for," Martin declares. "They found us."

Much to everyone's surprise, the Confederates invite the cellar-dwellers to come out of their confinement and have something to eat.

"What should I make of this?" Martin asks himself as Confederate soldiers and their "prisoners" join in a hearty dinner.

"No words I preach will ever capture this moment, when enemies sit down together and share a meal."

Watercolor by Gettysburg artist Tom Rooney

Winebrenner house

NIGHT WORK

Wow, what a day! I'll bet everyone is glad that it's over.

That's for sure, LIAM, but for ANNA GARLACH, the night has its own adventures.

The Shriver House

Anna Garlach **smiles to herself,** wishing her father had been home to see it! She was thinking of her mother earlier that day. Mother had grabbed the young Confederate sharpshooter when he entered the house and began to head up to the attic.

"Stop right there!" Mother shouted as she took hold of his cartridge belt, and pulled him back toward the front door. "You'll only bring fire upon this house and the children in it." And back out he went onto Baltimore Street.

Anna, who is 18, has never seen her mother in such a state. Hammering from the cellar soon brings her back to reality. Completing the work that Mother and brother Will began during the night means that Anna is the designated babysitter for her six-month-old brother, Baby Frank.

"Mother," says 12-year-old Will, "here is the last of the planking that I found in Father's shop." Catherine Garlach, up to her knees in water, is just completing a makeshift floor in the cellar to accommodate her family. The runoff down the southern slope of Baltimore Street from last week's rain prevents them from being safe and dry.

Will pulls the planking through the cellar entrance as quietly as he can. "I can hear Confederates talking inside the Schriver house," he reports to his mother. "They must be in every empty building on this side of town."

"They won't get into this house as long as I'm here," replies Catherine, taking the first plank from Will. "It will be getting light soon, so no more trips to Father's shop. You might be mistaken for a Reb."

"Mother," Will asks, "when the cellar is ready, do you think we might just take a peek from the garret window?"

The day was still a blur to Tillie Pierce.

Standing in front of Jacob Weikert's barn, southeast of Gettysburg, she watches the passage of still more Union artillery. A cannon is forced to stop and wait for repairs. The others are pulled by six horses at a trot, while the men run alongside. The rutted road causes the limber and caisson to throw off stones in every direction. Tillie hears the distant sound of fighting into the early evening, but since then the only noise is that of thousands of Union soldiers marching at quick-step on Taneytown Road. Only on occasion do they stop and move to the roadside to allow artillery to pass.

Tillie's long, late-afternoon hike on the first day had started from her home on Baltimore Street. Pushed along by the retreating Union soldiers, it was both exhausting and exhilarating.

"Hold on to my hands, girls," she shouts repeatedly to the two little Shriver sisters.

They follow Mrs. Shriver through a mass of disoriented soldiers.

Climbing up Cemetery Hill and through the Evergreen tombstones is the hardest part.

Their pace slows as they reach Taneytown Road, swing south through the fields, and finally arrive at the Weikert farmhouse.

"What is happening to my family?" thinks Tillie. She remembers the look of relief on her mother's face when she left with the Shrivers.

"And what will become of me, standing here safe and sound, away from the fighting? Perhaps this wasn't such a good idea after all. I'm missing everything!"

ELIZABETH THORN, *known as **"THE ANGEL OF GETTYSBURG,"** takes over **EVERGREEN CEMETERY** after her husband joins the Union Army in 1862. In sweltering summer weather, she buries over **100 BODIES** that are strewn around the **GATEHOUSE.** And get this—she's **SIX-MONTHS PREGNANT** and has three young children. Men are sent to help but soon skedaddle because they just can't take the heat!* ▶

Evergreen Cemetery Gatehouse

Elizabeth Thorn statue

∿CHAPTER 2

HOLD THIS GROUND

AT ALL COSTS

Little Round Top

GENERAL LEE AND HIS ARMY ARE ON A ROLL. They have pushed the Union forces back from Seminary Ridge. Now they must drive them from Cemetery Ridge on the other side of town.

If you could fly over it, the Union line would look like a fish hook. One end rests on Culp's Hill in the north and the other on Little Round Top in the south. The "hook" makes a turn on Cemetery Hill, closest to town. Lee will begin by striking both ends, but even Cemetery Hill will not escape.

Before General James Longstreet can begin the assault on Little Round Top, Union General Daniel Sickles moves his troops out toward the Emmitsburg Road. The Confederates strike this new, thin line with great force. The two sides fight over the Peach Orchard, through the Wheatfield, and up Little Round Top—over every inch of ground, back to where Sickles started.

When the Confederates press forward to Devil's Den, Little Round Top is empty of defenders! General Gouveneur Warren sees this, and orders everyone he can find to hasten to the top. It is a close call, but the Federals hold.

The Confederates try next to get around the side of Little Round Top. This is the very end of the Union line. Colonel Joshua Chamberlain and his men from Maine arrive in the nick of time, and save the entire left flank from collapse. The same story is repeated on Culp's Hill on the Union right, and Cemetery Hill, at the very neck of the fish hook.

By day's end, Lee's army has attacked both left and right. The Federals bend, but don't break. Wounded are everywhere—in barns, homes, churches—and in the streets, sharpshooters.

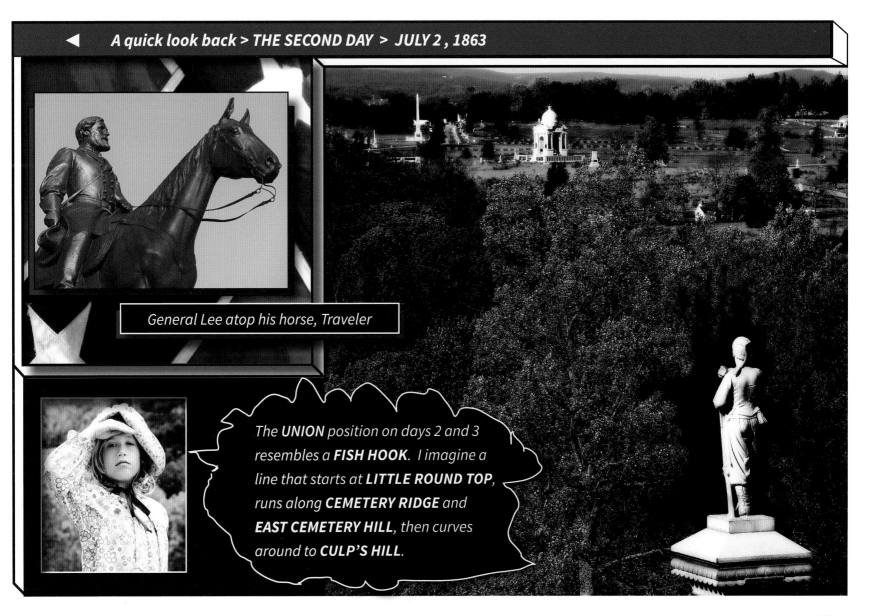

General Lee atop his horse, Traveler

The **UNION** position on days 2 and 3 resembles a **FISH HOOK**. I imagine a line that starts at **LITTLE ROUND TOP**, runs along **CEMETERY RIDGE** and **EAST CEMETERY HILL**, then curves around to **CULP'S HILL**.

LIAM, I feel sorry for all the wounded. Where do they go, and who takes care of them?

As we'll see, **JADEN**, a lot of incredible kids, like **SADIE BUSHMAN** and **TILLIE PIERCE**, have to step up and do incredible things.

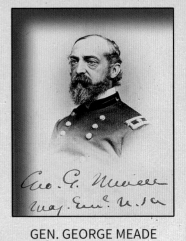

► *Awakened in his tent by one of **LINCOLN'S MESSENGERS** on the morning of June 28, 1863, **GENERAL MEADE**, known as "Old Snapping Turtle," thinks he is **UNDER ARREST**. Instead, he is told that he now **COMMANDS** the entire **ARMY OF THE POTOMAC!***

KIDS WHO DID THE IMPOSSIBLE!

GEN. GEORGE MEADE
ARMY OF THE POTOMAC

*GENERAL MEADE, just so you know, I was totally prepared to use my **ALLOWANCE** to spring you from **JAIL**.*

WHERE does LINCOLN FIND these guys?

THIS IS THE PLACE WHERE I WILL STAY

"What's happened to Mother and Father?"

Sadie Bushman asks herself, stirring a pot of broth in her grandmother's kitchen. The nine-year-old has lived on her Grandfather Bushman's farm for well over a day and a night. She fled there with her younger brother during the first day's fighting.

As soon as Sadie arrived that morning, the farm, located west of Rock Creek and behind the Round Tops, turned into a whirlwind of activity. The house and barn were transformed into a field hospital as wounded soldiers began pouring in.

She would never forget helping the surgeon who, having no one else, asked Sadie to hold a water cup to a wounded soldier's mouth while removing his shattered leg. It all seemed so long ago, but only yesterday!

Suddenly her thoughts are interrupted. "You should be elsewhere, little girl, anywhere but here," a corporal says while stoking the cooking fire. "This is no place for someone your age." On the contrary, whatever fear Sadie felt is long gone. Her job is here, tiptoeing among the wounded, helping them drink the broth she brings them. This is where Sadie wants to be.

Watercolor by Gettysburg artist Tom Rooney

ANOTHER ANGEL OF MERCY

Since late afternoon, Tillie has experienced a profound change from teenage schoolgirl to caregiver. After a quiet morning, the scene at the Weikert farm, located at the base of the Round Tops, becomes bedlam.

Soldiers rush past them to the front, then a torrent of wounded stream back to the farm. The house, and all the outlying structures, are taken over by Union medical staff.

At first, Tillie is occupied with ladling water to quench the soldiers' thirst and wet their bandages. Everywhere she hears the cries for help and the groans of pain. "What more can I do?" she wonders as darkness begins to fall.

Tillie notices movement in a corner of the basement. Holding her lighted candle in one hand and a water bucket in the other, she sees a wounded officer lying on the hay-littered cellar floor.

"**M**issy, where should we place this wounded soldier?"

the stretcher-bearer asks Tillie. She stands inside the barn among a sea of wounded, each waiting a turn with a physician to determine his medical fate.

74

"My name is Tillie Pierce, General. Would you like some water?"

"Yes, yes, please," is his soft response, "and please stay with me for a while."

"Of course," Tillie says, reaching down to tilt his head toward the ladle, "but only for a minute, so you can rest. I promise that I will come to see you first thing in the morning."

"Now don't forget your promise," the general replies. His head falls back onto a pillow of hay.

"No indeed," Tillie says as she walks back toward the cellar door. Her words disappear into the darkness, along with the light she carries.

"Hold the ladder still while I open the trapdoor,"

whispers Albertus McCreary to his younger brother who is a few steps below. Albertus has planned this adventure since noon, but has had to wait until Father finally went to bed.

Albertus McCreary *(reenactor)*

CLOSE CALL ON THE ROOFTOP

JADEN, who's the general Tillie's helping?

We'll have to wait to find out. Now keep your head down, LIAM. The night belongs to sharpshooters!

The second day of the Confederate occupation is nearly over. From the sounds of fighting in the afternoon and early evening, Albertus can only imagine the results. The Rebels who passed his home on High Street were too weary, thirsty, and hungry to chat with a teenager. But this only increased his curiosity.

The family porch is the only place Father allows the boys to go outside the house. An appearance by anyone, soldier or civilian, near the crest of Baltimore Hill, would draw a minie ball from a Yankee sharpshooter. Father calls the area a "kill zone."

The trapdoor squeaks as Albertus gives an upward push. "Let me get on the roof first," he quietly orders. Then he crawls into the darkness. Within moments, both boys are spread-eagle, flat against the roof.

"Look toward the Evergreen gatehouse," instructs Albertus. He notices Union troops moving among the gravestones. Then his eye catches a movement near the Shriver house, just one block below his vantage point. A Rebel squad is taking position, silent and purposeful.

Stretching his head a bit above the roofline for a closer look, Albertus hears a buzzing sound a mere instant before a piece of the chimney flies off.

"Get Down!" Albertus doesn't wait. He recoils in fear. A sharpshooter has him in his sights!

"That was too close," Albertus says to himself, sliding cautiously back toward the trapdoor. He motions to his anxious brother to follow. "Not a word of this to Father!"

∾ CHAPTER 3

IT'S ALL MY
FAULT

Photo by Taryn Kerper

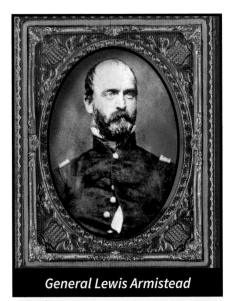

General Lewis Armistead

General George Pickett

GENERAL MEADE IS SURE THAT LEE WILL TRY

AGAIN, and he'll come straight toward the center. He's correct. At 1:00 p.m. a thunderous artillery barrage signals the start. A mile-wide infantry line, as many as 12,000 Confederates, march out from Seminary Ridge toward Cemetery Ridge. History calls it "Pickett's Charge." The goal is a clump of trees across an open field nearly a mile away. As the Rebels approach, Union artillery open fire, and the boys in butternut brown fall in rows.

General Lewis Armistead, with his hat raised on his sword, breaks through the line with about 200 Confederates. Not for long. Armistead is struck down. Pickett's charge is driven back with terrible losses. Cemetery Ridge is forever "the high water mark of the Confederacy."

Lee is a gentleman soldier. He rides out on Traveler to encourage the survivors. "It's all my fault," he says sadly. After the deafening roar that could be heard miles away, people in town and country feel a strange silence. Their battle—tending the wounded, burying the dead, restoring their homes, fields, and farms—has only just begun.

Photo by Taryn Kerper

IN THIS SECTION

Hold your fiddlestick, *LIAM!* There'll be more in the next chapter. Right now, the kids in town are huddled in their cellars. And those in the country are caring for the wounded.

► **CAMP FOLLOWERS** are mostly **WOMEN** and sometimes **CHILDREN**, too. They follow armies and help out in every way imaginable. They also transport goods and are even known to hide supplies under their skirts. Many are **WIVES** of soldiers, especially the poor who can't survive alone. They cook, wash, sew, and care for their injured husbands when needed.

KIDS
WHO DID THE IMPOSSIBLE!

*Has the word **"NAP"** been **INVENTED** yet?*

~ CHAPTER 4 WE WILL NEVER BE THE SAME

McPherson Ridge

Dr. Jonathan Letterman

◁ *Letterman (far left) and Staff*

THIS WILL BE NO ORDINARY FOURTH OF JULY.

The battle has ended. General Lee and the Confederate Army retreat in a heavy rainstorm. The wagon train stretches more than 17 miles. Yet, over 30,000 wounded soldiers of both armies remain behind. There are no hospitals until Dr. Jonathan Letterman establishes an organized camp on the edge of town. The local folk, even children and nuns, must tend the wounded, bury the dead, and destroy the remains of horses and mules. Debris is everywhere—piles of clothing, shattered trees, and broken fences. Most dangerous are the unexploded bullets and shells.

Watercolor by Gettysburg artist Tom Rooney

▶ **BASIL BIGGS** is an active member of the **AFRICAN-AMERICAN COMMUNITY.** He probably helps runaway slaves by transporting them at night to Quaker Valley, a slave hideout near Gettysburg. After the battle he assists **SAMUEL WEAVER** and exhumes Union bodies for reburial. He reportedly receives **$1.25** for each body. With well over **3,000 BURIALS,** he earns good money and uses it to purchase a new farm.

KIDS
WHO DID THE IMPOSSIBLE!

▶ **AFRICAN AMERICANS** fight for freedom in the Union Army but are segregated in death. It's not likely they'll feel welcome at the **NATIONAL CEMETERY,** so **BASIL BIGGS** and friends organize **THE SONS OF GOODWILL** to create a cemetery of their own. Eventually it's called **LINCOLN CEMETERY** in honor of the president who issued the **EMANCIPATION PROCLAMATION.** Biggs is buried here, along with thirty members of the **U.S. COLORED TROOPS.**

BASIL BIGGS, BASIL DIGS!

FATHER

BASIL BIGGS

DIED
JUNE 6, 1906
AGED
86 YRS. 5 M. 6 D.

CELEBRATION

"What's going on, Father?" asks Albertus McCreary as he slips his suspenders over his shoulders. He is just out of bed, expecting to repeat the pattern of the last three days: a quick breakfast of whatever food is left in the house, listening to the shouts of Confederates in the street, and then waiting for the sounds of artillery, which signal the family's return to the cellar.

"They're gone! The Rebels are gone! Must have left during the night," declares Father. He pushes the porch door open to look up High Street. Albertus brushes past him, running to the nearby corner.

"Here come our troops," someone announces, "marching toward the Square!"

Albertus hears the roll of drums. The Stars and Stripes appear just above the crest of Baltimore Hill. Each drumbeat, each step reveals a row of Union troops, then another and still another, marching toward him. "Is the army returning to Gettysburg?" shouts Albertus to a mounted officer.

"Just long enough to rest a bit before we chase Bobby Lee back to Virginia!" the officer shouts back. Albertus smiles to himself. The three-day battle he thought might never end is over, and on this special day, the Fourth of July! But at what price to Gettysburg, Albertus wonders, as he gazes down the streets one by one. The four churches he can see are filled with wounded. Dead soldiers and stacks of amputated limbs remain to be buried. Slain animals are pushed aside to permit access, but they rot just the same. Debris of the armies, more than he can imagine, is everywhere—clothing, leather straps, bedrolls, ammunition. It seems every house has a red square of cloth hoisted on a pole over its door, marking the presence of wounded inside.

"We will never be the same," says Albertus to his father. "Nor will our town."

Watercolor by Gettysburg artist Tom Rooney

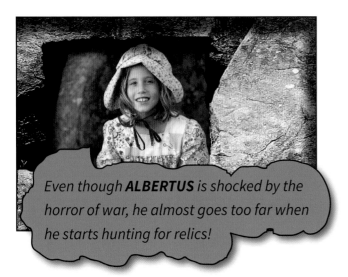

Even though **ALBERTUS** is shocked by the horror of war, he almost goes too far when he starts hunting for relics!

A DANGEROUS BUSINESS

"I've got to find a new hiding place for all this," Albertus whispers to himself. He crawls along the dark, dusty loft of the family carriage house behind the McCreary home.

The battlefield is filled with the leftovers of war. Albertus has collected nine rifles, three pistols, numerous bayonets, canteens, and other military gear that he discovered when he managed to sneak away from home. "I'm certainly not the only one doing this," he reassures himself. He imagines that every teenage boy in Gettysburg is engaged in the same activity.

The Union Army offers to pay anyone 13 cents per pound for lead recovered from the fields. As a consequence, Albertus and his friends spend nearly every day hunting for "spent" bullets on Culp's Hill or any of a hundred other battlefield locations.

Today's hunt has Albertus back on Culp's Hill, where the heavy tree growth provides plenty of places for ammunition. It also provides cover from his competing friends.

Yesterday he hit a mother lode! He quietly explains his discovery to his brother. "I was near Stevens Knoll where our boys had an artillery battery. I found three large shells that were full of bullets. Very carefully I unscrewed the cap ends, just like I saw the Union sergeant do when he found a shell near the McMillan House. I filled each shell with water from a canteen I had picked up. I removed the bullets, about 16 from each shell. Nearly six pounds of lead!"

As he tells the story and displays his bravery to his brother, Albertus recalls a pledge he made. Stick to bullets in the future. He made this promise after a friend found a shell and tried to hasten the process by striking it against a rock. The shell exploded! Albertus and other schoolmates had the unpleasant task of carrying their bleeding friend back into town before he died from his gruesome wound.

"Perhaps I'll just use my hatchet to cut out bullets embedded in the trees," Albertus says to his brother. "I can sell them to the tourists!"

Stevens Knoll

I feel so sad about **ALBERTUS'S** friend.

War is terrible, **JADEN**. Imagine how it looks to **TILLIE PIERCE** as she makes her way home with the little **SHRIVER** girls.

TRAIL OF TEARS

"Girls, stay very close to your mother and me,"** instructs Tillie. They leave Taneytown Road and turn into a field leading back toward Baltimore Street. Tillie Pierce is finally heading home! It is Tuesday, July 7. She has spent six days nursing Union wounded at the Weikert Farm. She remembers Union General Stephen Weed on the night of July 2. Weed's dying wish is that Tillie will return to his side at first light. She keeps her promise, but, sadly, she finds the general dead. "But what will I find when I get home?" she asks herself, suddenly fearing for her parents and three brothers.

What she sees in front of her provides no assurance. The rain that began on the Fourth of July leaves mud everywhere. Splintered trees mar the landscape. Fences not used for firewood were toppled by the fighting. The girls have to watch every step. Occasionally, they come across bodies of fallen soldiers, too ghastly to gaze upon. More common are the dead horses, bloated and grotesque in their death pose. Everywhere one looks are discarded weapons, bedrolls, empty ammunition boxes, and unimaginable amounts of debris. An unyielding stench has settled over the entire battlefield.

"I so hope and pray my family is spared all this," Tillie says to Mrs. Shriver.

Now within sight of home, Tillie wonders about the red flag over the front door. Her thoughts are interrupted when the door opens.

"Tillie is home!" her mother shouts, wiping her hands on her apron and running toward her only daughter.

"Is everyone safe, Mother?" asks Tillie, passing through the front door, home at last.

"We are all well and so very happy to have you with us again," Mother replies. "Each day is a little better than the one before, now that the armies are gone. But first I must introduce our visitor from Minnesota. Colonel Colvill is staying in your room. He was severely wounded when he and his little band charged the Rebs as they were about to break through the Union line on the second day of fighting. He's nearly six-and-a-half feet tall, and we had an awful time fitting him into a bed. Don't be alarmed at his wounds." She pauses a moment, then adds, "Later you can tell us if there were any wounded at the Weikert farm."

Tillie smiles as she thinks back to all that she experienced and the many soldiers she nursed. Never would she have thought possible all she saw and did.

Lydia Ziegler (reenactor)

Thousands of wounded, **JADEN**, just like **COLONEL COLVILL**. They fill every available building in town.

That makes me wonder about our friends, **LYDIA and HUGH**. Their home, the seminary, has been full of wounded since the first day.

LYDIA LENDS A HAND

When Hugh and Lydia Ziegler return to their **home** from the safety of Two Taverns, they find wounded soldiers in and around the whole seminary building. Everything the family once possessed is either damaged or destroyed.

"No time to worry about that," Mother declares. "We need to help these poor boys." She immediately sets about becoming the cook. The soldiers begin calling her "Mother." Lydia does her best to help. "God bless you, my girl!" the soldiers call out.

"Can I help you?" Lydia asks an old couple she meets one afternoon.

"We've walked all the way from Chambersburg to find our son Charlie," the man replies.

"Our four other sons already died in the war."

Lydia leads them to the third floor where they find Charlie, dying.

"How they cry," Lydia observes as the mother bends over the boy, "but I hope they get some comfort from their last moments together."

Figures of wounded soldiers in the Seminary Ridge Museum

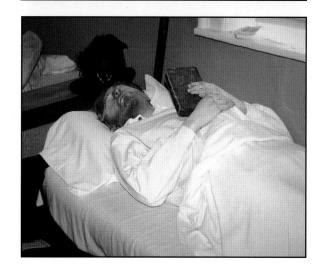

A GRIM REAPER

What a tough job for a young girl like **LYDIA**. I'm glad I don't have to do it.

But could you ever do what **LYDIA'S** brother, **HUGH,** does? He's still a kid, for goodness sake!

Hospital
Seminary Ridge

Despite his very young age, even Hugh is put to work, and what terrible work it is! His job is to help remove amputated limbs from the surgical area. He takes them to an ever-higher pile of decomposing flesh at the rear of Old Dorm, eventually to be buried.

It all looked so very exciting at first. Hugh recalls how he sneaked out on the first day and headed toward McPherson Ridge until he heard his first cannon barrage.

Now, before he returns to the hospital, he looks at all the wounded spread around the seminary grounds. He says to himself, "So, this is what the soldiers mean when they talk about 'the Butcher's Bill.' It's the grim count of casualties after battle."

"Days End July 1st"

Painting by Dale Gallon

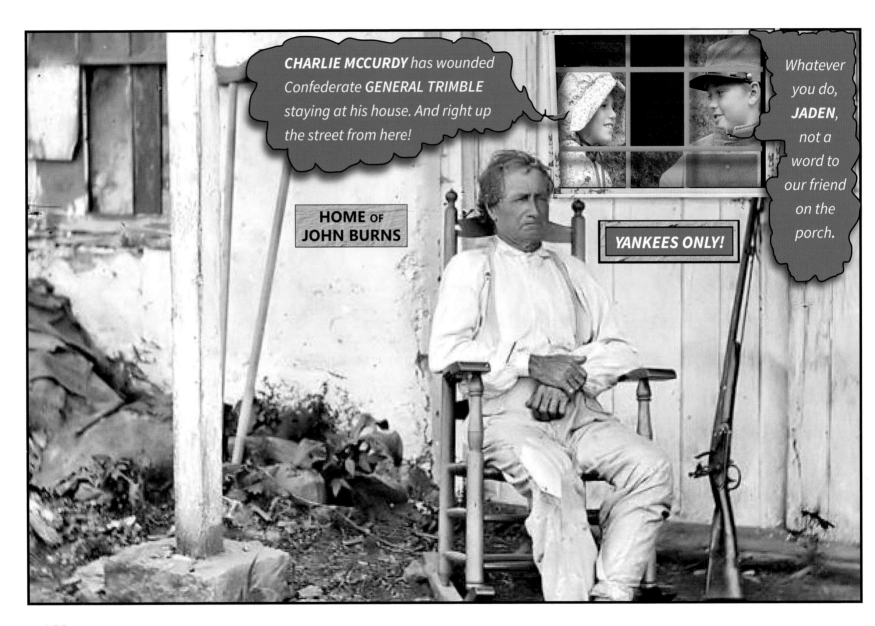

A DIFFERENT SORT OF HOUSE GUEST

General Isaac Trimble

Once the McCurdy family returns to their **Chambersburg Street home,** Charlie's mother is as thoroughly engaged in the care of the wounded as is most every woman in Gettysburg. In fact, a Union officer who suffers from a severe arm wound occupies the room next to Charlie's for days. Their newest patient arrives one evening in an ambulance and proves to be very special.

He's not just a Confederate. He's a general!

"Charlie, please say hello to General Isaac Trimble," says Father, introducing their patient after several days of recuperation have passed.

Gettysburg Railroad

"How do you do, General," says Charlie politely, "and how is your leg wound?"

"I'm sorry to report, Charlie, that my leg had to be amputated," the general replies, "but I have only one complaint. If the doctors had taken the leg a year ago when I was wounded the first time, there would have been nothing left to hit, and I would not have fallen into Yankee hands! Still, I am well, thanks to your parents' very fine care."

Charlie's father and the general share the same peacetime profession. Mr. McCurdy is president of the Gettysburg Railroad. So he and General Trimble, formerly the chief engineer for the Baltimore and Ohio Railroad, have many stories to share. His stay is less as a wounded prisoner and more an entertaining guest.

As the days pass, some local Union zealots complain that Trimble is living in comfort while many Federal soldiers suffer in primitive conditions. As a consequence, the general is forced to return to the seminary hospital, a disappointment to Charlie and even more to the general!

LIAM, I've been struck by a **SPLINTER!**

Seriously, **JADEN**, I think we can save the **FINGER!**

FIELD HOSPITAL

PLEASE BE SEATED. PERMANENTLY.

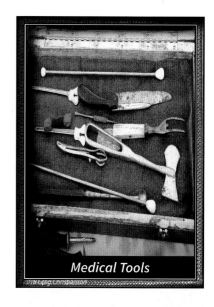

Medical Tools

Surgeon

▶ Civil War doctors: A leg up on the field?

More like a **LEG OFF.** You don't want to get sick at Gettysburg—and certainly not wounded. **HEALING** and **MEDICINE** lag years behind the technology of killing. **DOCTORS** are unaware of the **GERM THEORY** and **ANTIBIOTICS** don't exist. Some medicines can be poisonous and infections run faster than the Federal retreat on the First Day. For serious injuries, the best your doctor can do is use **CHLOROFORM** as an anesthetic and amputate your limb. Three of every four surgeries are **AMPUTATIONS.** And although it saves many lives, an astounding **TWO-THIRDS** of all fatalities during the Civil War are due to **INFECTION** and **DISEASE.**

NELLIE NO MORE

CHARLIE McCURDY is sure going to miss GENERAL TRIMBLE, but BILLY BAYLY is going to miss his horse, NELLIE, even more.

NELLIE

Tell ME about it!

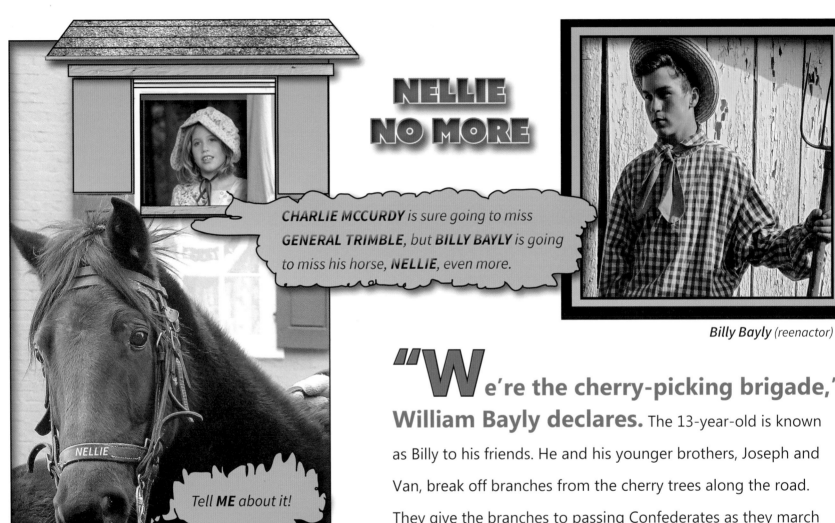

Billy Bayly (reenactor)

"**W**e're the cherry-picking brigade," **William Bayly declares.** The 13-year-old is known as Billy to his friends. He and his younger brothers, Joseph and Van, break off branches from the cherry trees along the road. They give the branches to passing Confederates as they march southward toward Gettysburg where the battle rages for a second day.

The boys have a secret. The fourth member of their group is a Reb and a deserter. The family has taken him in and given him civilian clothes. They don't use his name. They call him "Cousin." It's a risky game the boys are playing, but Cousin goes unrecognized. The Confederates have bigger things to worry about.

Billy can barely remember all the adventures leading up to this day, but he knows that everything is changing, including himself. He is a country boy, not a town-dweller like Albertus McCreary or Charlie McCurdy. His life during the battle on a large farm near Table Rock, a few miles north of Gettysburg, is much different than theirs. For instance, they must protect the family's livestock, especially their valuable horses.

It all begins in late June. Billy and his father, Joseph Bayly, "skedaddle" when they hear rumors of a Rebel advance into Pennsylvania. "How glorious is war," Billy thinks to himself as he is tossed on the back of Nellie, a beautiful chestnut mare. She is his favorite horse, and was Father's gift to Billy's only sister before she died of diphtheria. Billy's excitement grows when a young friend gallops up. "What's going on?" shouts Mr. Bayly.

"Cousin" and *Van* (reenactors)

The young man replies, "You'll soon find out if you don't hurry. The Reb cavalry is on my heels. You better git or you'll be got!" And away he rides.

Billy and his father think they have enough time to stop and rest at a farm along the way, but they are overtaken by four Confederate troopers. "We're trapped!" Billy whispers to his father.

The Confederates begin to haggle with the farmer, so Father says firmly, "Quietly, William. Follow me!" They sneak away, head for the barn, and mount their horses. "Quick! Into the woods!" They jump the fence into the meadow and gallop toward the trees. And they don't stop until they are certain the danger has passed. "The Rebs are headed for York," Father says. "We'll be safer at home."

Mother is pleased to see them, but not happy to see the horses. "William and I will hide them on the lower level of the barn," Father says. "We'll take food to them at night when no one is watching."

Their worst fears are realized on July 1. Great numbers of Confederates swarm over the farm as Union forces fall back from Barlow's Knoll and McPherson Ridge. Some of the Southerners seem to be in no hurry. They tease Billy and his mother about their opposition to slavery and how the Rebs will whip the Yankees.

"These boys are in good spirits," Mother says. "I think they're stragglers. If we feed them, they might not be

so anxious to get into the fight. That will help our cause."
She asks Billy to round up the chickens, but he develops a
sore foot in the chase.

"You don't amount to a hurrah as a chicken catcher," says
one Reb, laughing, and pulls out a pistol. Before long,
Confederate guns dispense with all the chickens.
Billy sees other Rebs running helter skelter over the fields.
"They're after our sheep!" he shouts. Shots ring out again.
Sheep are dropping everywhere.

"They're a mighty hungry bunch," Mother replies. "They're
eating up the bread as fast as I can bake it. Pretty soon I
expect our cows and pigs will go missing, too."

Night comes, and Billy wonders who's going to feed Nellie
and the horses hidden in the barn. Father has gone to
town and left him in charge of the family. He falls asleep
thinking, "This war is beginning to wear on me."

Suddenly there's a knock at the kitchen door. "Come
with me, William," Mother commands, with concern
in her voice. At the door is a very young man in a gray
uniform, not much older than Billy.

"My company was cut to pieces," the young Confederate says, unsure of how they will receive him. "I never want to see another battle. Will you take me in?"

"You'll find some beds stored in the garret," Mother
replies. "In the morning we'll find you some clothes.
Then you can help William and the boys with
their chores."

As the next day wears on, Billy climbs the roof above
the porch. As the sounds of battle reach fever pitch,
he complains to himself, "I'm not getting to see the

big show. All my time is taken up with *do this* or *do that*." From his perch he hears nothing but flash and roar, like a storm with sharp, angry crashes of thunder. The porch shakes and the windows rattle, but he can't tell which side is winning. His watching comes to a sudden halt when three Confederate officers appear. They ask Mother to put them up for the night.

As he goes to his own bed, he passes the guest room. The door is slightly ajar. He glimpses swords and pistols in their holsters. Suddenly, he gets an idea. Grab the weapons and capture the officers! "But what will happen to my family if I'm caught?" he asks himself, and passes by.

When morning dawns, Billy notices that things have changed. "Good news and bad news" is his mother's greeting. "Chickens, sheep, pigs, cows, and steers are all gone, but the battle must be over. The Rebs are in a poor mood, and they're moving out in the direction they came from."

As one Confederate passes by, he swears at Father. An angry Billy is about to lunge at the soldier when Cousin grabs him and whispers, "Don't! It'll be bad for you and even worse for me." When Billy calms down, it dawns on him that a former Reb has just saved him from the Rebs. Just then a Confederate leads three horses out of the barn, including Nellie. Alert soldiers

found the hiding place during the night. Mother implores the officer to leave the mare behind. "She was our dear daughter's pet," she pleads. The officer throws down the reins and declares,

"Madam, if you have a parlor, lock her up in it, for you will lose her if you don't." With that, he vanishes with the other horses.

The joy and relief last only a moment. The trooper returns. "My commanding officer won't let me do it," he says. "I despise this business. My own brother was shot down at my side this very morning. I could not stop to give him a kind word."

Billy turns away, not wanting to watch as Nellie disappears into the distance. Nor does he want to watch his younger brothers, who are fighting back tears.

"No, boys," Billy would like to say if he could only find his voice, "war is not glorious."

～CHAPTER 5

AFTER-WORDS

PRESIDENT ABRAHAM LINCOLN ARRIVES

DAVID WILLS IS A GETTYSBURG ATTORNEY. He becomes aware that bodies still lie in open fields or in shallow graves. He is moved by the sight and asks the federal government to establish a national cemetery. Even before the cemetery is completed, he plans a dedication for November 19, 1863. He invites the famous orator Edward Everett to give the main speech and asks President Lincoln to deliver "a few appropriate remarks."

PRESIDENT ABRAHAM LINCOLN ARRIVES at the Gettysburg train station on November 18 and is greeted by a large crowd. Together they walk to the Wills' home on the Town Square. Before the president goes to bed, he puts a few final touches on his address.

The next day, Everett takes two hours to deliver his oration. Lincoln takes only three minutes. Yet his "remarks" become the most famous address in American history. Later in the afternoon, Lincoln joins John Burns, a Gettysburg hero, for a short walk to the Presbyterian Church. The president has a brief meeting with supporters from New York. Soon afterward he's back at the train station, bids everyone farewell, and returns home to Washington, D.C.

Watercolor by Gettysburg artist Tom Rooney

113

If I could go back in time, **JADEN**, I'd find a way to meet **ABE LINCOLN** and help him polish up the **GETTYSBURG ADDRESS**.

The good news, **LIAM**, is that you **ARE** back in time and the **PRESIDENT** is here. The bad news is that until recently you thought the **GETTYSBURG ADDRESS** was a Diner.

LINCOLN'S HEIGHT often causes smiles and chuckles. Lincoln rides a normal-sized horse in the parade to the **NATIONAL CEMETERY**, but some complain that it looks like he's riding a mule. Not the horse's fault—just that the president's feet almost touch the ground. Later during the walk to the **PRESBYTERIAN CHURCH**, observers laugh to see poor old **JOHN BURNS**, short of stature, almost running to keep up with the **LONG-LEGGED PRESIDENT!**

KIDS
WHO DID THE IMPOSSIBLE!

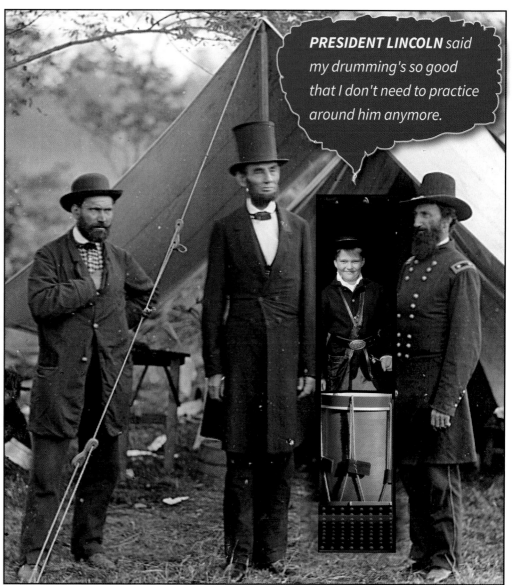

115

Holy lanky **LINCOLN**, I think I see the **PRESIDENT!**

A PRIVATE MOMENT WITH THE PRESIDENT

"What a day to remember,"

says sixteen-year-old Liberty Hollinger, known as Libbie to her friends. She, her sister Julia, and other classmates take turns gazing out the second-story window above York Street. They watch the milling crowd in the Square below. But they are looking for someone special.

They are visiting the home of lawyer Robert McCreary. Their perch gives them a "birds-eye" view of all the activity at the David Wills residence across the street.

President Lincoln is staying there while he's in town for the big occasion. "We've been invaded a second time," Libbie says to herself.

This one brings thousands of people for the solemn dedication of the Soldier's National Cemetery. Soon the parade to the cemetery will assemble. Right now, however, the crowd is far from reserved. They are in a holiday mood under a near-cloudless November sky.

Since Lincoln arrived yesterday evening, excitement grows by the hour. Bands play, politicians speak, trains and stagecoaches arrive with more and more visitors. But Libbie's eyes are on the Wills House, hoping for a glimpse of the president. For hours, the girls witness Pennsylvania's Governor Curtin meet and greet everyone who enters—a handshake here and a backslap there.

Liberty Hollinger (reenactor)

With each passing minute, however, a suspicion grows that the president has slipped through the Wills Law Office and into the comfort and quiet of the Harper house next door. "I guess I'll not see him after all," says Libbie quietly to no one in particular.

She gives her place at the window to Julia, who almost immediately cries out, "There's the president!"

Yes, there he is, pacing back and forth in a second-floor room. His hand clutches a paper. His expression portrays a focus on something much more solemn than the festivities outside. "What must our president be pondering," Libbie asks herself. "And why the sadness etched in his facial features?"

Maybe it's because he's about to make the most famous speech in American history. But there's no way for Libbie, or even Abraham Lincoln, to know this. Not yet.

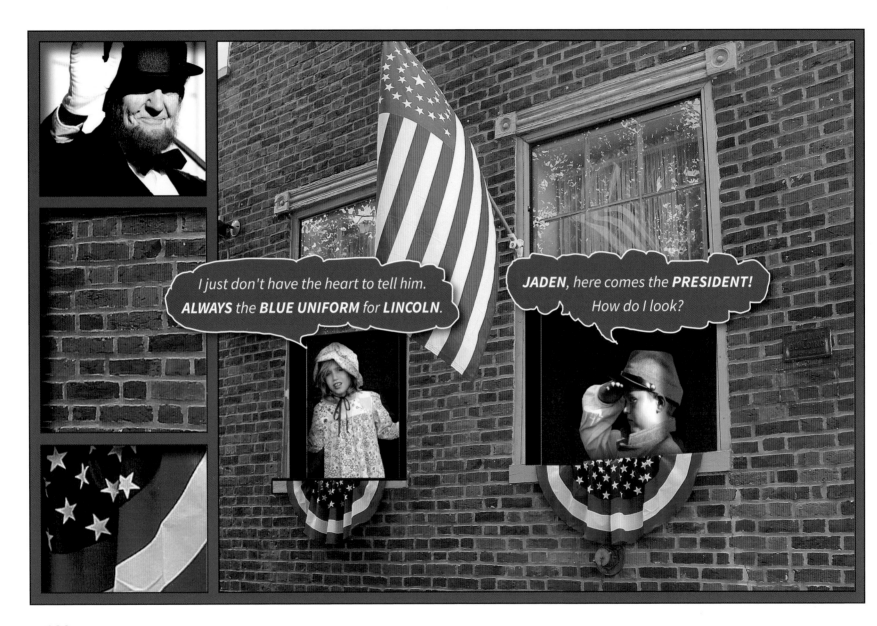

120

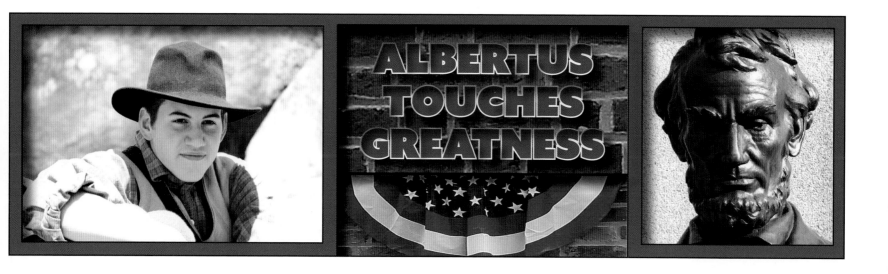

ALBERTUS TOUCHES GREATNESS

It seems like Albertus McCreary

is jostled and pushed in every direction. Never one to miss an adventure,

he has to make his way through the immense crowd outside the

Presbyterian Church. The situation is even worse when he squeezes inside

the main entrance.

Albertus is on a mission! For the past two days, he and everyone else in

Gettysburg have been in a near frenzy. First the arrival of President Lincoln,

then the official procession from the Square to and from the Soldiers' National

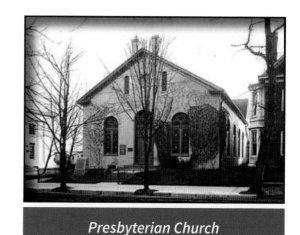

Presbyterian Church

Cemetery. He takes all this in and thinks it is nearly over. Then he hears that Lincoln will make a surprise visit to the Presbyterian Church. It's right across from his home.

The tumult produces an uproar. "We've not seen this since the first day's battle almost five months ago," Albertus muses. The president's entourage swells with every step as it comes down Baltimore Street. Father spots Lincoln first.

"There's the president!" he shouts to Albertus. And look who's with him. Old John Burns, the hero of Gettysburg."

The always-curious Albertus is drawn through the cross currents of the crowd and straight toward the church. Inside, the throng is so dense that he can hardly see what is happening, much less see the president. Minutes upon minutes pass as he clings to his position next to a pew, hoping against hope that Lincoln has not already left by another door.

The audience at the front starts to leave, rising from their pews. As they do, Albertus turns to the aisle. Suddenly, seemingly out of nowhere, there stands a tall, gaunt figure. His calm face brightens for a brief moment as his eyes meet those of the startled youngster. Without hesitation, Albertus holds out his hand.

"Mr. Lincoln, will you shake hands with me?"

"Certainly, young man," is the kindly reply. A strong handshake and the Great Emancipator disappears again, swallowed up in the crowd.

Watercolor by Gettysburg artist Tom Rooney

David Wills House

WILLS HOUSE, full house!

The **DAVID WILLS HOUSE**, now a **NATIONAL PARK MUSEUM**, is the former home and law office of the man who is instrumental in creating the **NATIONAL CEMETERY** and inviting **PRESIDENT LINCOLN** to the dedication. The president stays in the Wills House on **NOVEMBER 18** and puts the final touches on his **GETTYSBURG ADDRESS**. In addition to the president and the main speaker, **EDWARD EVERETT**, who have their own rooms, a whopping **37 GUESTS** stay here! Rumor has it, no one sleeps well. They all snore .

LIAM, did you know **LINCOLN** delivers the **GETTYSBURG ADDRESS** in less than **THREE MINUTES?** Today it can be read by children and adults in **87 LANGUAGES**.

Hmm. I wrote a **BOOK REPORT** shorter than that and my teacher said it was **UNTRANSLATABLE . . .**

The **LINCOLN GETTYSBURG ADDRESS MEMORIAL** is possibly the only monument in the world that is dedicated to a **SPEECH!**

SENIOR·VICE-COMMANDER-IN-CHIEF
OF THE G.A.R.
ALBERT WOOLSON OF DULUTH, MINNESOTA
THE LAST SURVIVOR

Just think, JADEN. There are 410 cannons, 148 historic buildings and 41 miles of roads on the battlefield—not to mention 1,320 monuments and markers. And every one of them has a story to tell.

Kids, Parents, and Teachers: Let's GROW together!

Did you know that out of the 620,000 soldiers who lost their lives in the Civil War, only about half were ever identified?

Now you, your family, or class can honor the fallen by having a tree planted in their memory through the **LIVING LEGACY TREE PLANTING PROJECT.** Each planted tree is geotagged and loaded onto a website where you can access pictures and other information about each fallen soldier.

Sponsored by **The Journey through Hallowed Ground Partnership,** we want to plant 620,000 trees along **The Journey through Hallowed Ground National Scenic Byway** (Route 15) from Gettysburg to Charlottesville, VA. The route stretches 180 miles over four states where many of the major Civil War battles were fought. **The Journey through Hallowed Ground** is working with the **NATIONAL PARK SERVICE, ancestry.com** and **fold3.com** to document the soldiers' stories.

WE HAVE NAMES

With your help, we can have 620,000 trees planted and growing by 2063, the Civil War Bicentennial!

SUGGESTED READING

SUGGESTED READING FOR YOUNG ADULTS

Anderson, Tanya. *Tillie Pierce: Teen Eyewitness to the Battle of Gettysburg.* Twenty-First Century Books, 2013.

Butzer, C.M. *Gettysburg: The Graphic Novel.* Bowen Press/Collins, 2009.

Catton, Bruce. *The Golden Book of the Civil War.* Adapted for young readers by Charles Flato. Golden Press, 1961.

Fritz, Jean. *Just a Few Words, Mr. Lincoln: The Story of the Gettysburg Address.* Grosset & Dunlap, 1993.

Herdegen, Lance J. *Union Soldiers in the American Civil War.* Savas Beatie, 2018.

Hughes, Mark. *Civil War Handbook: Facts and Photos for Readers of All Ages.* Savas Beatie, 2019.

Hughes, Mark. *Confederate Soldiers in the American Civil War.* Savas Beatie, 2017.

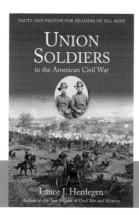
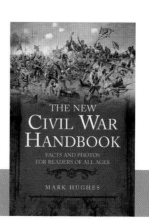
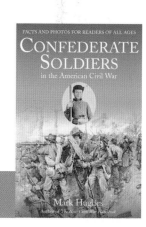

Klein, Lisa M. *Two Girls of Gettysburg.* Children's Books, 2008.

Martin, Iain C. *Gettysburg: The True Account of Two Young Heroes in the Greatest Battle of the Civil War.* Sky Pony Press, 2013.

Miller, Bobbi. *The Girls of Gettysburg.* Holiday House, 2014.

O'Connor, Jim. *What Was the Battle of Gettysburg?* Grosset & Dunlap, 2013.

Ratliff, Thomas. *You Wouldn't Want to Be a Civil War Soldier! A War You'd Rather Not Fight.* Franklin Watts, 2004.

Tarshis, Lauren. *I Survived the Battle of Gettysburg, 1863.* Scholastic, 2013.

Venner, William Thomas. *Young Heroes of Gettysburg.* White Mane Kids, 2000.

SUGGESTED READING FOR ADULTS

Adelman, Garry E., and Timothy H. Smith. *Devil's Den: A History and Guide.* Thomas Publications, 1997.

Boritt, Gabor. *Gettysburg Gospel: The Lincoln Speech that Nobody Knows.* Simon & Schuster, 2006.

Catton, Bruce. *Gettysburg: The Final Fury.* Vintage Books, 2013.

Christianson, Gerald, Barbara Franco, and Leonard Hummel, Editors. *Gettysburg: The Quest for Meaning.* Seminary Ridge Press, 2016.

Coco, Gregory A. *A Strange and Blighted Land. Gettysburg: The Aftermath of a Battle.* Savas Beatie, 2017.

Coddington, Edwin. *The Gettysburg Campaign: A Study in Command.* Simon & Shuster, 1997.

Coleman, W. Stephen. *Discovering Gettysburg.* Savas Beatie, 2017.

Frassanito, William A. *Gettysburg: A Journey in Time.* Scribner, 1975.

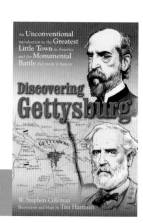

Gramm, Kent. *Gettysburg: A Meditation on War and Values.* University of Indiana Press, 1994.

Guelzo, Allen. *Gettysburg: The Last Invasion.* Vintage Books, 2014.

Hessler, James A., and Wayne Motts. *Pickett's Charge at Gettysburg: A Guide to the Most Famous Attack in American History.* Savas Beatie, 2015.

Hoch, Bradley R. *The Lincoln Trail in Pennsylvania: A History and Guide.* Penn State University Press, 2001.

Mackowski, Chris, Kristopher D. White, and Daniel T. Davis. *Fight Like the Devil: The First Day at Gettysburg.* Savas Beatie, 2015.

Mackowski, Chris, Kristopher D. White, and Daniel T. Davis. *Stay and Fight it Out: The Second Day at Gettysburg.* Savas Beatie, 2019.

McPherson, James M. *Hallowed Ground: A Walk at Gettysburg.* Zenith Press, 2015.

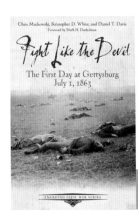
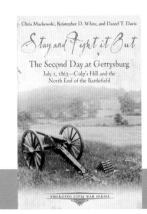
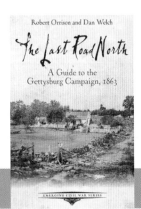

Orrison, Robert, and Dan Welch. *The Last Road North: A Guide to the Gettysburg Campaign, 1863.* Savas Beatie, 2016.

Petruzzi, J. David. *The Complete Gettysburg Guide.* Savas Beatie, 2009.

Pfanz, Harry W. *Gettysburg: The Second Day.* University of North Carolina Press, 1987.

Reardon, Carol. *Pickett's Charge in History and Memory.* University of North Carolina Press, 1997.

Shaara, Michael. *The Killer Angels.* Modern Library, 2004.

Wittenberg, Eric J., and J. David Petruzzi. *Plenty of Blame to Go Around: Jeb Stuart's Controversial Ride to Gettysburg.* Savas Beatie, 2006.

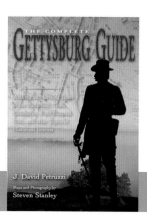
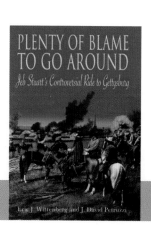
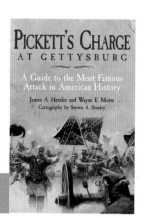

Friend to Friend Masonic Memorial

It is rather for us to be here dedicated to the great task remaining before us— that from these honored dead we take increased devotion to that cause for which they gave the last full measure of devotion—that we here highly resolve that these dead shall not have died in vain—that this nation, under God, shall have a new birth of freedom—and that government of the people, by the people, for the people, shall not perish from the earth.

Abraham Lincoln

November 19, 1863

acknowledgments

Extraordinary thanks to my family • Larry Donnelly • Kerie Horan-Noll • Steve Morgan • Terry Fox • Kelly, Marissa, and Abby Sandoe • April Schilpp • Lisa Peduzzi Konopka • Alan Natali • Matt and Lily Crowner • Michael Crowner • Lora Bertram • Maddy Gaydon • John, Becky, and Alivia Colgan • Tara Rhodes • Sierra Lookabill • Stacey, Al, and Kassidy Oussoren • Fred, Noe, and Lucas Oberholtzer Hess • Alex Aumen • Susan Colestock Hill • John Messeder • Jake Boritt • Jill Ogline Titus • Civil War reenactors the world over • Gettysburg National Military Park • Adams County Historical Society • Gettysburg Seminary Ridge Museum • Victorian Photography Studio, Gettysburg, PA • StoneSentinels.com • Gettysburg Heritage Center • Mr. G's • Bradley Hoch • Crystal Griffiths • Michigan Joe • Steve Zimmerman • Bill Sharpe • John Zervas • Terry Latcher • Phil Wolfe • my contributors: Tom Rutherford, Gerald Christianson, Tom Rooney, Dale Gallon, and Taryn Kerper • my publisher, Theodore Savas, for seeing the possibilities in this project, and Sarah Keeney for guiding it through to completion.

AUTHOR &
CONTRIBUTORS

GREGORY CHRISTIANSON

▶ *is an author and photographer, lives in Gettysburg, and has been walking the fields near his family home since he was a child. The idea for this book came about when he realized there were few books suitable for younger readers and families. Greg is the former publisher and editor of the award-winning* Unsung Hero Magazine, *and the author of the well-received* The Reconciliation of All Things. *He keeps fit by tramping the battlefield in search of the perfect photograph and by coaching and playing soccer at every opportunity.*

GERALD CHRISTIANSON

▶ *is Professor Emeritus of Church History at United Lutheran Seminary, Gettysburg, and co-editor of GETTYSBURG: THE QUEST FOR MEANING.*

TOM RUTHERFORD

▶ *is a resident of historic Bethlehem, PA, and a retired bond portfolio manager and teacher. A Licensed Town Historian in Gettysburg, his interests include teaching, military history, and fitness pursuits.*

TOM ROONEY

▶ *is an eminent watercolorist who is best known for scenes of historic Gettysburg. He graduated from Gettysburg College and for many years served as a paramedic at Gettysburg Hospital.*

DALE GALLON

▶ *has painted over 300 historical images since 1980. Each image is a history lesson on canvas. He is especially proud of the ten paintings that the Gettysburg Seminary Ridge Museum enlarged into murals.*

layout and graphic design

• Gregory Christianson

photo credits

• Gregory Christianson

with additional photos by Taryn Kerper (78-79; 81), and others in the
public domain courtesy of the Library of Congress (10, lower left; 14; 19; 20,
upper right; 26; 31, lower right; 34; 48; 71; 80; 83; 86; 100; 101, upper right; 103; 115; 129; 130).

photo editing and manipulation

• Gregory Christianson

watercolor paintings

• Tom Rooney

oil paintings

• Dale Gallon

The modern photographs in this book are meant to capture the imagination. They may not
replicate in specific detail every place or person referred to, whether civilian or military,
including their units, ranks, uniforms, or costumes.

GETTYSBURG
KIDS WHO DID THE IMPOSSIBLE!

www.GettysburgKidsBook.com

www.Facebook.com/GettysburgKidsBook

Download a study guide free